Poetic Justice

Poetic Justice

Satirical verse from
The Globe and Mail

by **John Allemang**

Illustrations by Brian Gable

A FIREFLY BOOK

Published by Firefly Books Ltd. 2006

First printing

Publisher Cataloging-in-Publication Data (U.S.)
Allemang, John.
Poetic justice : satirical verse from the Globe and Mail / John Allemang ; Brian Gable.
[ ] p. : ill. ; cm.
ISBN-13: 978-1-55407-229-3 (pbk.)
ISBN-10: 1-55407-229-8 (pbk.)
1. Verse satire, Canadian (English). I. Gable, Brain. II. Title.
III. The globe and mail /John Allemang.
811/.6 dc22 PS8601.L4446.P64 2006

Library and Archives Canada Cataloguing in Publication
Allemang, John
Poetic justice : satirical verse from the Globe and Mail / John
Allemang ; illustrations by Brian Gable.
ISBN-10: 1-55407-229-8
ISBN-13: 978-1-55407-229-3
1. Verse satire, Canadian (English). I. Title.
PS8601.L443P63 2006 C811'.6 C2006-902014-0

Published in the United States by
Firefly Books (U.S.) Inc.
P.O. Box 1338, Ellicott Station
Buffalo, New York 14205

Published in Canada by
Firefly Books Ltd.
66 Leek Crescent
Richmond Hill, Ontario L4B 1H1

Cover and interior design by Kathe Gray/electric pear

Printed in Canada

The publisher gratefully acknowledges the financial support for our publishing program by the the Government of Canada through the Book Publishing Industry Development Program.

For Sam

And malt does more than Milton can
To justify God's ways to man.

— A.E. Housman, *A Shropshire Lad*

Introduction

Deadline is such an unpleasant, unforgiving word. I became a journalist because the only way I was going to write was with that do-or-die frenzy, and while the deadline poems I push into being each week have produced moments of high anxiety, they wouldn't exist without the clock's creative compulsion.

I'd call it exquisite torture, but in a world where state torture has become an acceptable short-cut to the truth, I probably should choose my words more carefully. That's the world these poems inhabit, for better and for worse, and that old definition of poetry — emotion recollected in tranquility — has no standing here. When I write my poems, the feelings are still raw and there's about as much tranquility as you'd find in a sudden-death hockey game. Though they may appear to be highly rational little compositions, writing against the clock is a mad, frantic, impetuous thing to do — the rhymes and the rhythms are what keep me from falling off the high-wire.

Poetic Justice appears every Saturday in the Focus section of *The Globe and Mail*, Canada's national newspaper. It began rather suddenly on April 6, 2002, a week after the Queen Mother died — I remember the date because the ancient royal was my first subject.

A month or two before, I'd found myself proposing that I launch a new feature which I called, for lack of a sexier description, a news poem. (Actually, I was intending to suggest a daily sonnet, but some rare burst of discretion got the better of my completely unjustified valour.) The concept of a news poem wasn't completely new — Calvin Trillin wrote weekly verse about the political world for *The Nation* magazine and Tony Harrison filed poems to *The Guardian* from the war in Bosnia — but by newspaper standards and maybe even poetry standards, it had a certain ballsy originality. To my surprise, Richard Addis, then *The Globe*'s editor, embraced the idea. And that meant I had to start producing. The trouble was that while I'd read a lot of poetry, and always found myself gravitating to topical, conversational verse like Byron's *Don Juan*, Vikram Seth's *The Golden Gate* and

Ovid's *The Art of Love*, I'd never managed to write any. Ignorance, or at any rate innocence, is rarely seen to be a disadvantage in journalism.

As the weeks went by, I kept waiting for this mysterious woman they call the Muse to give her go-ahead. As luck would have it (this is a callous business), the Queen Mother finally died and my editor Cathrin Bradbury came to me with her fateful words of journalistic inspiration: "I think you should start this week." We worked out some ground rules that I've held to ever since: The poems are about a personality in the news, they have fairly dependable rhymes and rhythms, and they aim to be comprehensible — pretty conservative stuff, except that I think the result argues otherwise, and not just because of the politics. In any case, I don't mind being called prosaic: George Orwell's line about good prose being like a windowpane is always in the back of my mind when I turn my phrases, and I'll gladly sacrifice lyricism, avant-gardedness and imagistic introspection if I can get closer to his twinned ideals of clarity and justice. The funny bits are mine.

Since the poem has to appear in the Saturday paper, the weekly rhythm goes something like this: I scour newspapers and news websites for likely subjects starting on Tuesday, and I e-mail my editors three to five possibilities with a short note about the tack I might take — e.g., "Laureen Teskey does a reverse Hillary Rodham." Because the Focus section is a mix of newsy features and topical columns, they will shoot down some of my suggestions right away if they're being covered in other stories. A few of my front-page favourites that looked promising as the week began are bound to feel worn out as the weekend draws nearer, others will seem premature in the greater scheme of things — let the scandal evolve another week or two, someone might say — and a few, while newsworthy, are just too mind-numbing for editors who've had their fill of Canadian politicians and their policies. Very rarely, when there's absolutely no one worthy of my angry iambics who hasn't been barbed two or three times before, I get to write about the latest attempt to find water on Mars or mess up Canada's national game.

Somehow we end up with a subject, unless we don't and the process spins out until Thursday, which is my usual writing day — close enough to Saturday to boost the adrenalin, far enough away that most disasters can be averted in time. In the less decisive weeks, I wake up on Wednesday or Thursday hoping a Hollywood icon has succumbed, or a televangelist has ordered a hit on a Latin-American politician, or some figure in the extended circle of White House cronydom has gone and done something foolish like ignoring a hurricane. As the clock runs out, the topic necessarily emerges, and I research it as thoroughly as time allows in *The Globe*'s database. Researching not only gets the facts right (which came in handy when my lawyer was able to give a point-by-point rebuttal during a hearing before the Ontario Press Council), but also helps to find the kind of salient detail that says more about my subjects than any angry rant I could come up with (the rapacious Dennis Kozlowski's poodle-shaped umbrella stand and cakes made to look like female nudes were a god-send). When you have only 150 or 200 words to work with, you need all the help you can get.

Though I usually write the poems on Thursday afternoons, and go back and forth with my nighthawk editor Carl Wilson long into the evening, there've been times when I've had to write them on Friday morning, on the understanding that I'd file by 10 a.m. Since the section I write for gets shipped to the printers at noon, this doesn't allow much wiggle room, or missed wake-up calls or dog-ate-my-diatribe excuses.

There are few pleasures sweeter than being struck (and that's what it feels like) by the perfect rhyme at 9:58 a.m., though I once took extraordinary delight in rewriting four lines of a poem (an innocent, playful poem) about a particularly litigious business magnate at 11:20 while *The Globe*'s lawyer waited on hold and my editor stood behind me saying, "I need it now." On the other hand, at about the same time on another Friday, I had to give up and cut my final couplet in a poem about Dick Cheney shooting one of his many friends because several of my superiors could not understand my particular brand of nuanced brutality.

I don't know how other poets work, but I write on a laptop — like the onrushing deadline, the emptiness of the screen and the blinking cursor keep me fixed to my chair, and I don't have to look at all the feeble rejects and hopeless cross-outs that a printed page retains. Somewhere within reach, just as a crutch, I keep a list of words pertaining to my subject that might usefully end a line, and occasionally I'll even test a few rhymes in advance as a work-avoidance strategy. I don't use these much, but it's always comforting to know they're there, and there's no denying that in the writing of this kind of late-breaking verse, a chance rhyme is as likely to prompt an idea or an argument as vice-versa. This sheet of paper usually turns into my scratch pad as I'm searching for something, anything, that will rhyme with Ignatieff, and by the time I'm done it's covered with desperate scrawls of the moon/ June/swoon variety and numerous half-formed couplets that went nowhere. Like all poets, and dreamers in general, I really can't stand to be interrupted by telemarketers — if only they knew how hard it is to recover that free-floating feeling, the dreamy ecstasy of rhyme finding rhyme.

When I started writing these poems, we (the collective newspaper brain trust that always gets excited by titles for new columns) decided on the name Poetic Justice. For a while I thought that both parts of the title were a little bold — these were mostly simple one-syllable rhymes in chatty iambic tetrameter, and how often has justice been served in verse? But now I see this odd form of rhythmic rage and metered laughs as up to the task of dealing with the daily cruelties, hypocrisies and idiocies, while still leaving room for a few rhymes of farewell for Kate Hepburn. "The world is a comedy to those that think, a tragedy to those that feel." I'd like to believe that poetry has both sides covered.

The Poems

In Hindsight: Maher Arar

The shame that overtakes the mind
In those of us who think we're kind
But hold our tongues when things go wrong —
"They must know better," that old song —
Is what we grasp in place of grief
To mourn the passing of belief.

Canadian telecommu-
nications engineer Maher
Arar was arrested in New
York on suspicion of links
to al-Qaeda and taken
by the CIA to a prison
in Syria where he was
repeatedly tortured. He
was released after a year
without being charged.

You think you know just who you are.
But then you face Maher Arar,
And all self-knowledge turns to doubt.
The torture that he talks about,
The dark nights in that stinking cell...
Could I have sent him straight to hell?

"Can't be too careful." So they said.
"The terrorists who want us dead
Don't honour law, so how can we?
And some must pay to keep us free."
We nodded while they went too far,
And saved us from Maher Arar.

But here's the lesson taught by shame:
The next time we won't act the same.
To save ourselves, we must do more
Than keep our peace in time of war
And let them tell us why and how.
Just one more thing — the next time's now.

Same-Sex: God Weighs In

The problem with omnipotence
Is this: You just can't fold your tents
And migrate to some distant place
Untainted by the human race,
Where no one vainly takes God's name
Or plays the power-glory game —
For even when you try to hide,
They still demand you be their guide,
The universal know-it-all,
Forever at their beck and call.

Right — same-sex marriage. Here's the thing:
If two men want to wear a ring
And do what married people do,
You won't catch this God shouting, "Boo."
Our mission statement up above
Is, "How can you go wrong with love?"
But what do I know? I'm just God,
A deity without a bod,
Who can't tell pious gay from straight
Or see why love should lead to hate.

So, not much brimstone, or much fire.
To you who think the issue's dire,
I must seem like a total fraud
And nothing like Isaiah's God,
Who steered his values to the right
And like George Bush, preferred to fight
The infidels who went astray.
I'd rather turn the night to day
Than force each he to find a she —
But then, no one elected Me.

Just Watch Me: Memories of Pierre

He flaunts it still, that Trudeau charm,
Which made us overlook the harm
His arrogance could do to us;
But now, post-mortem, all the fuss
Is how his charismatic gaze
Advanced his womanizing ways,
And made Pierre our JFK —
Part-time PM, full-time roué.

As sycophants and acolytes
Chew up his life with fond love-bites,
It's Margot Kidder's kiss-and-tell
That makes their pious tributes sell,
While Bob Rae's sister's steamy nights
Eclipse all talk of Charter rights —
Provided that you're good in bed,
Who cares what History's judgment said?

The nation's bedrooms aren't the place
For prudes and scolds to make their case,
So Trudeau told us, more or less;
But from his rule we must digress,
When one who boasted of his brain
Chased Funny Girl and Lois Lane,
Used sex when power failed to thrill,
And got his way: He taunts us still.

Pope Wanted

The fallible need not apply,
And those for whom the needle's eye
Might seem too narrow to pass through
(Which is to say, the wealthy few,
Whose riches win our churches' love
But seem to displease God above)
Cannot reign in the Holy See.
We're looking for humility,
A man who during Holy Week
Will wash the bunions of the meek,
And not complain that he's too good
To scrub where Jesus said he should —
But not so humble that he can't
Keep up his predecessor's rant
And swear the oaths that John Paul hurled
Against the -isms of this world.

It helps to wear a Cardinal's hat,
The scarlet cap which tells us that
You're holy, celibate and male,
Like He who bore the cross's nail —
But less inclined to speak of love
When sinners need a good hard shove.
Tough talk's the currency in Rome
And here, beneath St. Peter's Dome,
You'll let the world know when it's wrong,
Which means, of course, your faith is strong
And any doubts you may have shared
Will, post-election, go unaired.
We know that money's not the lure,
But, so you know, the church is poor —
Just damn the wicked, flee from taint,
And when you're dead, we'll call you Saint.

The First Casualty: Jean Charles de Menezes

One bullet missed. Split-second fire
Makes even seasoned cops perspire
And hit the shoulder, not the head,
With freedom's well-intentioned lead.
Still, seven bullets found their mark
On skin the experts thought was dark,
Or dark enough to pass for bad
According to the leads they had,
And if he'd hadn't quickly died
He might have been a suicide,
With Lord knows what tricks in his pack
To prompt their unprovoked attack.

How dare, they ask, he run away,
Or wear that jacket on a day
When no upstanding English lad
Would be caught dead so overclad?
The innocent, as we all know,
Can figure out war's fashion show —
When some armed man tells them to stop,
A voice within says, "Plainclothes cop,"
But when the rule of law's ignored,
The rule of force claims its reward,
And those who lack stiff upper lips
Die in cold blood on subway trips.

Jean Charles de Menezes was an innocent Brazilian stalked and killed by police following the London bus and subway bombings of July 2005.

Valediction for Jean Chrétien, 2003

As Sea Kings crash into the waves,
And ministers go to their graves
Proclaiming that they did no wrong,
As Martinites light up a bong
To toast their triumph (and your fate),
And leaks spring from the ship of state
Whose plank you're walking just in time,
Accept, dear Jean, this farewell rhyme.
I know that culture's not your scene
(Except the sculpture meant to bean
The crank who gate-crashed Sussex Drive
And fled your welcoming high-five),
But don't confuse this verse with art —
Like you, it shoots straight from the heart,
And unlike, say, *The Life of Pi*,
It's aimed right at the little guy.

The little guy — I love that phrase.
Of all your talents to amaze,
Those skills you use to steal a vote
Or make light of a damning quote,
It's image-crafting where you're best.
Le petit gars — who would have guessed
You'd power-lunch chez Desmarais,
And silence mobs with pepper spray?
Le style, c'est l'homme: The style's the man.
You run the Hill like Vince McMahon,
And crush those who stand up to you —
Remember Flag Day, when you threw
That little guy down to the ground?
Sure, you're some fighter, pound for pound,
But statecraft is a finer art
Than chokeholds straight from Hitman Hart.

Still, who are we to give advice?
If Mitchell Sharp can't make you nice,
And voters wouldn't throw you out,
You must know what it's all about:
Corruption and the GST
Mean less than caucus loyalty,
And when the opposition gains,
Ship Gagliano to the Danes.
And yet, you scuppered Conrad Black,
Resisted George Bush on Iraq,
Then held off power's push and shove
To win approval for gay love —
Who knew you'd find, in sex that's queer,
That principle's not just veneer?
Your motives? I won't try to guess —
We both know who's left with the mess.

Coach, Cornered

Now listen up, you kids out there —
Nobody said this game is fair.
You want a piece of Cherry's mind?
Don't act so shocked when he's not kind
To nancy boys and Euro-sucks
Whose faces never stopped no pucks.
What makes a true-blue hockey guy?
The willingness to lose an eye
And offer up what's in his cup
To earn the coach's proud thumbs-up.

They say the game has passed Don by?
This queer world needs his straight-guy eye
To bring back hockey's manly arts
And rip out all those bleeding hearts —
What tie goes best with blood and gore?
This ain't a sport, it's civil war,
So throw away that full-face shield
To make a level battlefield,
And then, when Cherry speaks his mind,
The blind will truly lead the blind.

Heeeere's Osama!

Like Michael Jackson running wild
And showing fans his latest child,
Or women who'll do anything
To try to steal *The Bachelor*'s ring,
Like poor Mick Jagger, still on tour,
Bin Laden craves the limelight's lure.

Too bad Osama's quest for fame
Can't end on some dumb TV game,
Where his desire to show who's best
Would not involve death for the West,
And like a vapid B-list star,
He'd save his ranting for Bill Maher.

But now he leaves us with no choice:
We have to hear that breathy voice
As he proclaims our coming doom
From what Bush promised was his tomb —
Just when you hoped the guy was dead,
His ego's begging to be fed.

Celebrities don't like to die.
Like Elvis spotted eating pie
At some forlorn off-ramp café,
They just refuse to go away,
Or make space on life's gravy train
For upstarts like Saddam Hussein.

This terror biz is awfully cruel.
Like rock and roll, you prove you're cool
By trying to launch another hit
When *People* says it's time to quit.
Osama, you weren't born to run —
Your time is up, go have some fun.

Write tell-all books about your god,
Make infomercials for *jihad*,
Tell Oprah how your kidneys feel,
And help Nigella cook a meal.
Then maybe, as your time runs short,
You'll end your days on *People's Court*.

Johnny Carson (1925–2005)

The box for idiots and boobs,
The brainless mess of wires and tubes
That makes stupidity a sport,
And gives the ship of fools its port,
Became much sharper when he spoke —
Not just the standard Carson joke
That cleared away the daily fog
In breezy bursts of monologue
(Though, truth to tell, his rapier wit
Could seem a scripted show-biz bit),
But more the knowing sidelong glance,
The raised-eyebrow, seat-of-the-pants
Delight at filling in the dots
With sudden late-night afterthoughts.

He walked away. "Who needs TV?"
He seemed to say — as ego-free
As when he occupied the chair
And said more with his knowing stare
Than lesser hosts whose non-stop gab
Makes interviews seem smash-and-grab.
Jay Leno serves up tepid gruel
Compared to Johnny's sense of cool,
And though he had his share of bores
(Think Tiny Tim, all those Gabors,
And stand-ups from some vaudeville past),
One quality will make him last:
Immune from stardom's worst disease,
He lacked that deadly need to please.

Those Bush Girls

It's time to cast off childish things —
The tapped-out kegs, the late-night flings,
The rap sheets gleaned from one-horse towns —
And put on de la Renta gowns
That make the world a proper stage
For Texas twins who've come of age.

Where once your photos graced the tabs
(All glassy-eyed and flabby abs),
Your glamour shots from this month's *Vogue*
Reveal a state that's far from rogue:
Instead of winding up in jail,
You're Page 1 in *The Globe and Mail*.

You've traded in your fake IDs
For selfless, save-the-world CVs,
And left behind your low-life haunts
To serve as campaign debutantes —
Who knew your zeal to help your Dad
Could make the Olsen twins look bad?

If strapless gowns and made-up eyes
Are what it takes to humanize
A man who sends kids off to fight,
Then you two have turned out just right:
Good girls don't ask the reason why,
But pose and smile while others die.

Survival Strategy

Rejoice, sad people of Darfur!
Though civil war has left you poor,
And made your women fear the nights
When darkness mocks your human rights,
Our one-time-only giveaway
Means help should soon be on its way.
Thanks to the Commons' civil strife,
You'll now be safe from torture's knife
And spend your lives in peace, not war,
If we can just bribe Dave Kilgour
To give Paul Martin his high-five,
That lets both us and you survive.

Let no one say the Grits don't care:
Our scores of troops will soon be there
In stylish blue peacekeeper caps
To help the locals read their maps
And show off Roméo Dallaire
To make the whole thing seem more fair.
Of course, with our minority,
We can't supply a guarantee
That all this aid is going to last
Beyond the time the votes are cast —
But meantime, wretched of the Earth,
Please rest assured, we know your worth.

In the far-off days of Paul Martin's precarious minority government, a last-minute aid package for war-ravaged Darfur was cobbled together to win the support of a crucial independent MP.

The Mulroney Transcripts

It's not so much the inner man,
Pale skin beneath the perma-tan,
That Peter Newman's tapes reveal,
But more the dark side of each deal,
Which outwardly made Brian glow
But deep down bruised his frail ego.

He loved to swear, and had to hate
Each traitor, poseur and ingrate
Who fed his insecurity
And went from friend to S.O.B.
The moment Newman took his call
And taped his set-it-straight tell-all.

But aren't these unspooled truths a fraud
For what's kept under wraps from God:
Why did he warble *Irish Eyes,*
His bland gaze filled with wild surmise
That joining Reagan's serenade
Would mean his name would never fade?

It pains us to rewind, and yet,
It's better that we don't forget
The expletive-deleted side
Of those who take us for a ride
By acting out the statesman's role
To fill the blank tape of the soul.

The New Mrs. Harper

Conservatives who long for change
Will not think it the least bit strange
That Stephen Harper's wife's last name
Is, post-election, not the same.
Farewell to Martin? "Teskey" too,
And those who crave the old-as-new,
Tradition branded as reform,
Hail Laureen's move back to the norm
Where no one gets to call her Ms.
And Harper's wife's more clearly his.

The Teskey thing worked out quite well
In softening the old hard-sell,
And like her motorcycle's roar
Made Stephen less the Tory bore
Who'd take away the right to choose.
But when he wins, Laureen, you lose:
Your independence got him votes
So now he needs a spouse who dotes
And doesn't try to be his peer
Or bring to mind Maureen McTeer.

As chatelaine of Sussex Drive,
Who needs much more to feel alive?
While Mr. Harper climbs the Hill
To pass some family-values bill,
The Mrs. gets to play First Wife
And live the model married life.
It's true, Laureen, you're made for more
Than greeting hubby at the door,
But women must stand by their man
To honour power's master plan.

Business Class

When greed was good, he got away
With making poor shareholders pay
For yachts and blowouts by the shore
That gave the lie to "less is more."
But now the lonely CEO
Is left with just the video
Of birthday treats bought for his wife
That cost him what remains of life,
Plus memories of past excess
To make his hard time seem much less.

In Attica's drab prison greys,
He recollects those golden days:
The shower curtain worth six Gs,
A David, made of ice, that pees
Not water but free-flowing booze
(It sure seems like a lot to lose),
A poodle-shaped umbrella stand,
Those well-oiled, muscled boys who fanned
The guests, flown to some far-off spot
To prove the guilty can't be caught.

And then things change: Does it seem fair
That Tyco's fall guy has to bear
A punishment to suit our times,
Far from the climate of his crimes?
A man whose concept of great food
Is cake shaped like a female nude
Cannot adapt to jailhouse swill,
And if you take away the will
To have some fun with fiscal frauds,
We'll lose all faith in Wall Street's gods.

Dennis Kozlowski, party guy and free-spending CEO of Tyco International, was sentenced to 25 years in prison for stealing $170-million from his company and manipulating its share price for another $430-million windfall.

The Art of War

War's ways have changed — you know it's true
When U.S. soldiers passing through
The cradle of the ancient world
Would rather see their flag unfurled,
Or make secure a Baghdad road,
Than plunder Hammurabi's code.

What used to be the perks of war,
The loot that justified the gore,
The art that grunts and brass both stole
When getting rich was fighting's goal,
Has been devalued. Now it's oil
That winning armies seek as spoil.

While Halliburton's profit swells
(The contract's signed to fix the wells),
And Kirkuk's saved for SUVs
(Cheap gas is one of freedom's keys),
The art that Rumsfeld doesn't need
Is sacrificed to freedom's greed.

"Who wants an old sarcophagus?
We've licked Saddam, so why the fuss
About old pots and tarnished jewels?
What's liberation? No more rules.
Free people make the odd mistake,
And won't love art just for art's sake."

All property is theft, it's said.
So rob the living and the dead,
And do your patriotic deeds:
By looting, plant free-market seeds
That one day, when the troops have gone,
Might turn into the next Enron.

Give and Take

*"Liberality lies less in giving liberally than in
the timeliness of the gift."*
      —Jean de la Bruyère (1645–1696)

Testimony from Montreal ad executive Jean Brault in 2005 exposed the Chrétien government's flag-waving sponsorship program as part of a kickback scheme designed to enrich the Liberal Party.

It's good, at last, to hear Jean Brault
(It rhymes with: "Please pay Chrétien's bro'")
Confess that, glimpsed behind the scenes,
Democracy's a hill of beans,
Where those who long for private perks
Find all they need in public works.

Those threats from separatists? All gone,
And in their place, *pays* as pawn
For phony patriots who bleed
The country dry to quench their greed,
And touch their friends up for a mil'
So bloated Grits can have their fill.

How strange that liberal means "free,"
Since Liberals expect a fee
And seats at every backroom feast
To keep our run-down freedoms greased —
For liberty, it now seems clear,
Means how much you can skim each year.

Far off in Rome, Paul Martin prays
For better men and better days.
But once he sees off John Paul II,
It's back to Parliament's screw-you,
For no words in St. Peter's dome
Can lead his party's lost soul home.

The Runaway Bride

According to the all-news script,
The breathless TV world was gypped
When fears for Georgia's kidnapped bride
Were dashed with this update: "She lied."
How dare Jen Wilbanks interfere
With TV addicts' right to hear
The news unfolding as it should:
The body, say, found in the wood,
Suspicions falling on the groom,
The cameras' vigil at the tomb
While preachers praise the almost-wife
And anchors ruminate on life.

Two weeks of ratings down the drain,
And all because this not-quite-sane
(But quite unslain) bride played a hoax
On simple scandal-loving folks.
The Michael Jackson trial lacks spice,
The new Pope's got a heart of ice,
And Baghdad's blood's so yesterday
Beside this missing fiancée,
Who broke the rules of breaking news
And so must face its stern "*J'accuse.*"
Too bad you ran away and lied —
They'd treat you better if you'd died.

Our Sympathies

Apologies for this week's blast —
The Taliban is quite aghast
That through some simple oversight
Your children died in broad daylight.
You know our war is not with you,
But just with the unholy few
Who aid the foreign infidel.
It's them we meant to send to hell,
But now and then, through some dumb glitch,
The wrong blood trickles down the ditch,
And those who always feared our laws
End up as martyrs to the cause.

We might ask why your kids were there,
When they should be inside, at prayer.
And note, we're not the only ones
Whose missteps kill off first-born sons:
The PLO and IRA
Both bombed their own kind day by day,
Believing that the gains you make
Can justify the odd mistake.
And when it comes to friendly fire,
Great Satan's built the highest pyre —
The means we all use for our ends
Have trouble sorting foes from friends.

But still, we do the best we can.
Remember, we're the Taliban,
And frankly the *mujahedeen*,
While strong in faith and very keen
To wave guns on the nightly news,
Should not be trusted with a fuse.
Our lawyers say we lack intent,
That it was all an accident —
But we're not here to shift the blame:
Like Pete Rose with the Hall of Fame,
We take a deferential stance
In hopes you'll give war one last chance.

The Good News

It's true that God, though full of thoughts
On mortal sins and thou-shalt-nots,
And why a pew's no place for shorts,
Does not have much to say on sports.
Preoccupied with Adam's rib
And why St. Peter told a fib,
He failed to damn the DH rule,
And lets kids think tattoos are cool
Because the prophets in his pay
Did not foresee the NBA.

But what God missed, the Church has found
In baseball's sermons on the mound,
In football's wild Hail Mary pass
That's just as good as Sunday mass.
And when we doubt a sprinter's pee,
There's comfort in the Holy See,
Where keeping up with sports-page crimes
Helps modern popes move with the times —
When artificial turf's a sin,
Who needs those angels on a pin?

In 2004, the Vatican set up a sports department as a way to connect with contemporary culture and open up new possibilities for evangelization.

Liberation: Yasser Arafat (1929–2004)

What can you say of Arafat?
No measured, balanced this and that
Will catch the essence of the man
Whom death claims as an also-ran.

A fighter born to kill, not lead,
Who never wanted to succeed,
He'd rather triumph in disgrace
Than front-run in the human race.

Revered, reviled? It's much the same —
He finally lost his high-stakes game,
And if you seek his legacy,
It's death, stripped of all dignity.

A fleeting hint of compromise,
And Yasser took the Nobel Prize,
But all the peace he ever found
Lies buried in Ramallah's ground.

As death lays out its welcome mat,
What's left to say of Arafat?
That terrorism's superstar
Proved killing only goes so far.

The Flood

When "levees" turned up in her script,
And TV showed the dikes being ripped,
The sad-faced anchor blinked her eyes
And gravely talked of breached "Levi's."
A fate much worse than ripped-up jeans
Has overtaken New Orleans,
Where rule of law hangs by a thread
And there's no time to count the dead,
But still, the hack's faux pas seems right:
This was to be Tsunami Lite
For CNN and all the rest;
The USA, put to the test
By yet another hurricane,
Would rise above such Third World pain
And make the wind and rain a lark
Feared only in a trailer park.

That's how the weather's meant to go,
Fun filler for a dry news show,
Where TV cameras soak up spray
And gusts of wind blow roofs away.
But when those Levi's/levees burst,
And good-news days gave way to worst,
The weather took a different role:
Dark window to the human soul,
Revealer of some master plan
That shows there's none so bad as man,
Rebuker of the godly line
That lauds intelligent design.
The proof for Darwin? Check the muck,
Where life or death comes down to luck
While TV, our fair-weather friend,
Warns that some pictures might offend.

The Star-Crossed Lovers

On nature shows, the courting dance
Precedes the moment of romance;
When screen stars dance the old soft-shoe,
It means the breakup date's come due.
So Brad Pitt can't contain his love
For Jennifer, sent from above?
And she'll remain his caring friend
Until their days come to an end,
And all that beauty turns to dust?
So dies the perfect couple's lust,
In love notes culled from P.R. kits
That break the news: They've called it quits.

It's less like *Fight Club*, more like *Friends*
When *People*'s favourite marriage ends,
And though Brad never got his heir
(A nation mourns!), they still have hair,
And multimillion-dollar deals
To pass the time between nice meals
Where stars agree that fame's a bitch
And weddings just make lawyers rich.
But if you seek the Trojan colt
That somehow lured *Troy*'s star to bolt,
Don't blame it on celebrity —
Think Angelina, née Jolie.

"I have built a monument that will last longer than bronze," the Roman poet Horace declared of his work. That was easy for him to say — he didn't write about celebrity marriages.

Arnie the Barbarian

In *Terminator: Judgment Day,*
You never had to stop and say,
"If I don't kill this low-life freak,
Will soccer moms decide I'm weak?"
Death's simpler in your movie roles
Where no one stopped to check the polls,
When Conan made revenge seem sweet
And gangsters ended up dead meat.

Tookie Williams, an L.A. gang leader turned activist, was executed in 2005 after beleaguered Governor Arnold Schwarzenegger refused to commute his death sentence.

But now the swing vote plays a part
In firming up your hardened heart,
And you send Tookie to the grave
Because you've got a job to save.
"I'd like to let him off, I would,
But clemency's misunderstood
As weakness in the face of force,
So I'll just say he lacks ... remorse."

It took him quite a while to die.
Like you, he was a bulked-up guy,
Which made it hard to find the vein
That adds the killer to the slain.
And so you end as you began,
By proving you're no girlie-man:
While Tookie's muscles feed the worms,
Strong governors seek second terms.

The Good Soldier

A man who likes to give things thought
Should not have let himself be caught
By those who, when they're near the brink,
Prefer to act instead of think.
But Colin Powell got suckered in,
And now can't wash away the sin,
The made-up *casus belli* taint,
That tars the man who preached restraint.

If fools rush in where angels fear
To shift past first or second gear,
Then Powell by nature joins the gods
While George Bush contemplates the odds
Of where his shoot-first style will lead.
Except, complicit in the deed
To make sure Baghdad was attacked,
Powell played the fool — and still got sacked.

Blame loyalty, the soldier's curse,
A good man serving those much worse,
But don't send Colin your regrets —
Some years ago, he placed his bets
And skipped the Democratic queue
To cast his lot with W.
A soldier knows: Live by the sword,
And soon you'll find yourself being gored.

Lady Bountiful

Lord Black's great hero, FDR,
Would not have made it quite so far
If Eleanor, the wife he wooed,
Had blinded him with pulchritude.
Alas, the lesson never took,
And Barbara Amiel's practised look
Distracts her lustful golden boy,
Much like what Helen did to Troy.

Whatever things she seems to lack,
Just send the bill to Conrad Black:
The butler bowing at the door,
Smooth flights aboard the *Gulfstream IV,*
The frantic Palm Beach social whirl,
A champagne toast from Richard Perle,
Ball gowns from Paris in the spring —
The lady loves her jet-set bling.

Napoleon had Waterloo,
For Conrad? Heels from Jimmy Choo
That mesmerized his lady friend
And made his Lordship spend, spend, spend.
But beauty does that to a man:
Desire beats any business plan,
And who's to say it's so obscene?
Some babes are worth the guillotine.

Are You There, Stephen? It's Me, God

Dear Stephen Harper, down below:
A winter lacking ice and snow
Is quite a blessing, don't you think?
Unless, of course, your backyard rink
Looks much more like the ancient flood
That drowned Earth's sinners — sorry, bud.

But here's my point: It works both ways,
This blessing thing. And when you praise
This Lord you like to call your own,
And beg him for some short-term loan
To boost your latest Tory cause,
Don't bet you've sorted out my laws.

If you think Heaven heeds commands
To shape war's cruelties with its hands,
Your Christian soldiers might fare well,
Or then again, might go to Hell,
Depending on whose prayers I hear
And which believer has my ear.

It could be them. It could be you.
But think back to George W.,
And where his God-blessed schemes have led,
Before you consecrate your dead —
And then, I know, you'll think again
Before you take my name in vain.

Stardust

You know celebrity's no fun
When Paris Hilton says she's done,
And vows she'll ditch *The Simple Life*
To play the part of simple wife.
A girl can just take so much hype
Before she craves a diaper wipe
To wash away the filth of fame,
And freshen up the Hilton name:
You're not so proud of doing porn
The moment that your baby's born,
So Paris swears she'll change her gears
(Just give her one or two more years).

For stars, it's now the latest trend
To close fame's story with "The End."
Pam Anderson has said Finis
To all that stuff with Tommy Lee,
And shifts from TV's close-up lens
To focus on the plight of hens,
While former teen queen Katie Holmes
Now pores through L. Ron Hubbard's tomes.
She got religion through Tom Cruise,
And though some say it's just a ruse,
A new life has to start someplace —
So why not near a handsome face?

And what of Michael Jackson's fate?
It's true, according to the state,
He's free to take up his old ways.
But those were hardly golden days,
And *Thriller* seems too long ago
To keep fame's neon sign aglow.
But if he could display more tact,
His life might have a second act:
With children exiled from his bed,
And surgeons banished from his head,
He'll find the things the famous lack,
And then his life can fade to black.

Divine Intervention

Who doesn't miss the good old days
When God wiped out salvation's strays
Without a sober second thought,
Or critics shouting, Thou shalt not?
The faith that bred Pat Robertson
May not have had much time for fun,
But when it came to games of war,
Pat learned what retribution's for:
Take out the enemies of God
Wherever they may lurk abroad,
For no Lord worth believing in
Deems shooting socialists a sin.

And yet, when Pat launched his crusade
To undertake a holy raid,
And serve the cause of true belief
By killing Venezuela's chief,
Nobody lined up at his side —
So much for pious homicide.
What suits The 700 Club
Still seems extreme, and there's the rub:
Who knows, on any given day,
Which Christians rule the USA —
The ones whose God still preaches love
Or those who kill, blessed from above?

In a fit of inspiration, TV evangelist and Republican Party power broker Pat Robertson called for the assassination of populist Venezuela President Hugo Chavez.

Katharine Hepburn (1907–2003)

No kung fu kicks or sci-fi gear,
No tight pink dresses up to here,
No curves like Austin Powers' birds,
Just bright eyes and a few sharp words
Delivered in taut Bryn Mawr tones
That melted flesh from strong men's bones,
And made them try so hard to please
Kate Hepburn, more than some cute tease.

Before Botox and breast implants,
She swore off makeup, dressed in pants,
Scorned "moron sex" and didn't care
What Africa did to her hair,
Or that screen time with Cary Grant
Need be more than a sharp-tongued rant.
What makes her work still seem so fresh?
Kate Hepburn played with words, not flesh.

From there to *Charlie's Angels II,*
From *Adam's Rib* to Lucy Liu —
Sure, it's not hard to feel despair
And think the world's beyond repair.
Reese Witherspoon? The best we've got?
Blond hair can't match a well-turned thought.
Your best point, as Kate Hepburn knew:
Not hair, not legs, but point of view.

Yesterday's Man

The McCartney Marriage (2002–2006)

If Muddy Waters dyed his hair
Or Howlin' Wolf traipsed down the aisle
With some blond model half his years,
We wouldn't sneer. No one would care
Or say that it's completely vile
When old men won't confront their fears.

The difference here? We see our face
In Paul's. The strain to put off age
Comes too close to our masquerade.
Our lives decline at equal pace
But no one wants to leave the stage
While there's a chance of getting laid.

His act's become an oldies show,
An encore that can't let it be,
A cheery ballad trotted out
To help resist time's undertow
And strengthen our naïveté
When we should rediscover doubt.

His youthful bride can't stand his hair.
To make her Beatle end this lie,
The gossips say, she wants it grey.
But his persona's past repair.
So live together, and let dye —
Paul still believes in yesterday.

Al-Zarqawi's Lament

Intelligence sources
reported that Osama bin
Laden had asked Iraq
insurgency leader Abu
Musab al-Zarqawi to
expand his operations
to the United States.
A U.S. air attack in
June 2006 curtailed
his plans.

I bust my hump to do the job,
To make that ragtag Sunni mob
A fighting force beyond compare
And increase terror's market share,
With low-cost strategies designed
To profit all the Prophet's kind.
But when I think I've done enough
(Car bombs! Beheadings! Front-page stuff!)
To give the infidels a shock
And help bump up al-Qaeda's stock,
By turning 'round a certain loss,
I find I still can't please the boss.

"Zarqawi, global markets call,
We'll need you stateside by this fall."
And just like that, I have to go,
Deferring to the CEO
Who lazes in his restful cave
While I end up *jihad's* wage slave —
When meetings last till kingdom come,
I see the point of martyrdom.
So farewell to the kids and spouse,
It's time to gate-crash Bush's house,
But if I'm going to bust my ass,
I'm damn well flying business class.

The Martha Stewart Year
(A Courtroom Pastorale)

As hard as it will surely be
To spend Thanksgiving in a cell,
And not trim this year's Christmas tree,
Or hear the trick-or-treaters' yell
While carving pumpkins with dear friends,
I feel this is a better time
To make, as lawyers say, amends,
And expiate my so-called crime.

The winter season, as you know,
Is pretty bleak in household terms —
Beneath that ivory coat of snow
There's little but the lifeless worms;
The sunlight's gone, the days are short,
And soon the ducks will be *confit*,
So jail me now, I beg the court,
For spring's the best time to go free.

In winter one can hide away,
And map out kitchen-garden plots,
But as we near the first of May,
Manure and mulching steal my thoughts;
And just as migratory swans
Return to claim their northern nest,
So I'll trade long drab nights with cons
For springtime's tasteful house arrest.

Just Say *Oui*

When independence sounds a bore,
And old Péquistes seem too hard-core
To rouse Quebec's *jeunesse dorée*
Come referendum's judgment day,
It's time to trade the cut-and-dried
For *pure laine*'s wild-and-woolly side.
And so we get André Boisclair,
The *patriotes*' breath of fresh air,
Who with his queer and handsome eye
Is sovereignty's Designer Guy,
And separatism's cute soft-sell
For those who like their province *belle*.

It's true he did a line or two.
But those who long to rule *chez nous*,
Who can't forget some ancient slight,
Will pardon what he did last night,
And gladly let him renovate
Their "*Je me souviens*" licence plate
If he can bring down Jean Charest
With such a modern résumé —
He's lively, gay, a dish, drug-free,
And who needs more from sovereignty?
Just learn, André, to take a joke
The way you took those lines of coke.

The CSIS Guide to Syria

Damascus is a charming place
For spies who seek a change of pace;
The bad guys here are locked in jail
And no one's ever granted bail,
Which means no spook need be distraught:
You'll see no evil in this spot.

Where better for some R and R,
Once you've checked out Maher Arar?
The paperwork's no big deal here,
So sit and sip a cooling beer,
While someone from the CIA
Does all the heavy work each day.

They say St. Paul was blinded here,
But these days you have less to fear,
For when you look selectively,
You miss things you don't want to see,
And some thoughts should remain unsaid
In case your briefing notes get read.

But when your quickie tour is done,
And HQ says it's time to run,
It's nice to know you've done your bit
To make rendition more legit —
At CSIS, we pursue what's right,
So nothing wrong can come to light.

Opportunity Lost

If water once flowed over Mars,
They must have had some trendy bars
Where smart young Martians, acting hip,
Refused to take a single sip
Of ordinary H_2O,
Preferring some imported *l'eau*
That gave imbibers instant class
With stylish burps of high-priced gas.

If Mars once flowed with brooks and streams,
There must have been great hockey teams
That wowed sports fans from pole to pole
With every picture-perfect goal.
But then the fastest game there is
Became another Martian biz,
And fans with nothing left to cheer
All cried in watered-down lite beer.

If Mars was moister than the rest,
Could it have launched the urine test,
Or watched some guy make water wine
And think this madman was divine,
Or beat us all to acid rain,
And let ice caps go down the drain,
And planets die? We don't know yet.
Our ignorance keeps us all wet.

Brother of Jesus

In 2002, a small stone
burial box turned
up in Israel and was
immediately identified
as belonging to James,
the Anointed One's
lesser-known brother.

So let's see if we've got this right:
Some looters wander out one night
To make big money from the dead,
And going where angels fear to tread,
They find a box that holds the key
To Jesus' place in history.

It's like the Bible doesn't count.
Forget the Sermon on the Mount
And all the tales in Mark and John.
We'd sooner trust some clever con
And put our faith in those who steal
A box that seems so much more real.

Which James is it? Must be the one
Who's brother to the Lord's own Son.
So let's collect his DNA
And hawk Christ's gene pool on eBay,
Right up there with the olive leaf
That proves the Flood deserves belief.

Ideas are dreary, give us facts,
And much less Gospel, much more Acts,
More stylish portraits of the Bard,
Or Aristotle's rookie card —
And so Christ's life is turned to gold,
The greatest story ever sold.

Poli Sci 101

"Is this Toronto or Kiev?"
Thinks Michael Grant Ignatieff,
As protesters make him the bane
Of old resentments from Ukraine.
"I came here not to cause a stir,
Or prompt a search for any slur
That may, in some ironic way,
Have stained my brilliant résumé.
What fool would give up Harvard Yard
To see his reputation tarred
By splinter groups (well-meant, I'm sure)
Who lack my superstar allure?

"No, I've come to Ontario
To be the next Pierre Trudeau,
And show you how a well-formed brain
(Which, as I said, respects Ukraine)
Will make Etobicoke feel proud
When I say fancy words out loud —
And, just perhaps, my dishy bits
Can woo more voters to the Grits.
But if I'd wanted drag-down fights
About my thoughts on human rights,
As deft and nuanced as they are,
Do you think I'd have come this far?

When Liberals in the Toronto suburb of Etobicoke took a shine to Harvard professor Michael Ignatieff, a descendant of Russian aristocrats and a prominent backer of the Iraq invasion, he was challenged by Ukrainian-Canadians who said he had disparaged their heritage.

"It's true, back home in Cambridge, Mass.,
Left-wingers want to kick my ass
Because I made the case for war —
Who knew what Rumsfeld had in store?
Philosophers who would be kings
Must take their minds off higher things,
And though my thoughts soar high aloft,
Please don't think that my spine is soft —
But if we sometimes go astray
Because we see the shades of grey,
It's not designed to cause you pain.
(Did I say that I love Ukraine?)"

Chain, Chain, Chain

The world is full of lonely cells,
Where every chain and jail bar tells
A story of man's evil ways
Back in some far-off, far-worse days.

In Senegal, George Bush seems sad
That his ancestors once went mad,
And looted Africa of souls
To cut costs on their cotton bolls.

This place where men were turned to slaves
Is what a politician craves:
Some harsh words for a long-gone crime
Means black votes at election time.

But why stop at this branch of hell?
Go visit wise Mandela's cell,
And share the trials the great man bore.
Oh right, you can't — he hates your war.

These moral cleansings have their flaws.
You have to pick and choose your cause.
Deplore all wrongs and soon, you know,
You'd have to tour Guantanamo.

The Road to Hereafter:
Bob Hope (1903–2003)

"Fish don't applaud," Bob Hope once said,
Returning early from a cruise —
The silence from the ocean bed
Denied his power to amuse.

The wink, the gag, the knowing leer,
Could not exist without a crowd.
Like Mick and Keith, the time to fear
Was when the volume stopped being loud.

It's true that Hope was far from hip.
His jokes ("like air," admirers said)
Were little more than pause and quip,
And didn't ask much of your head.

He lived too long, the old man's curse.
The memory that won Hope's thanks
Looks back and sees a past that's worse,
The G.I. jokes by Danang's tanks.

His politics? Bad to the core —
A comic just can't be a hawk.
But give him this: Sent off to war,
He couldn't shake his urge to mock.

At death's door came a last request:
"Bob Hope, according to state laws,
You must now choose your place of rest."
Big wink. "Surprise me." Cue applause.

American Idol

Montgomery's a name we know,
A town where white men once said No
To those who broke the 'Bama rule
And risked their lives to go to school,
A place whose God could see no sin
In dining choices based on skin.
Much chastened, God is now less sure
Of right and wrong, so Judge Roy Moore
Stepped in to help pick up the slack:
To bring the old-time values back,
Montgomery's own demagogue
Installed a courthouse Decalogue,
And made the Ten Commandments' laws
The legal system's new lost cause.

The South, they say, has changed its ways:
The good old boys' quite bad old days
Have mellowed in the heartless sun,
And football's played by everyone.
But when you think the old extremes
Have been replaced by Krispy Kremes
And no one wants to stir up hate,
A lawless judge binds church to state,
And find cures for each social ill
In props from Cecil B. DeMille.
Feel free to build your Lord a shrine,
Just don't make justice too divine —
God knows how many wars are fought
To reinforce each thou-shalt-not.

In a crusade to restore Judeo-Christian values to public life, Alabama's chief justice Roy Moore installed a 2 ½ ton granite replica of the Ten Commandments in the rotunda of the state courthouse.

Royal Male

There's little point to brilliant rants
When no one's listening but your plants.
Take pity on the Prince of Wales
Who, like so many older males,
Has figured out where things went wrong
But can't find takers for his song
Of anti-modernist despair
Against the world of Tony Blair.

You'd think Camilla Parker-Bowles
Would satisfy his midlife goals
And keep the Windsors' aging heir
From tearing out his thinning hair.
But no, Charles needs an audience
To offer up due deference
And greet his words with loud applause
As he defies New Labour's laws.

Each night before he goes to sleep
Instead of counting rare-breed sheep,
He scrawls long letters to his foes
And steps on democratic toes
By saying the British farmer lacks
The largesse shown to gays and blacks,
Or that the fox deserves to die
To keep the feudal spirit high.

Surrounded by smug sycophants
He truly thinks he has a chance
To play a king behind the scenes
Or, at the least, ban GM beans
From tainting Britain's virgin soils.
Advice to Charles: When your blood boils,
Instead of fighting for your class,
Put down that pen and pour a glass.

Rock of Ages

With miracles, God picks his spots,
And while we all want lots and lots
Of great things to emerge from bad,
And doomed hopes quickly turned to glad,
The good Lord goes his own sweet way.
Sure, bend your knees and start to pray
That saving men trapped in the mine
Will somehow suit the Lord's design,
And loudly sing your favourite hymn
To capture his capricious whim,
Which sometimes saves men digging coal
And sometimes tips the Sugar Bowl.

But when you're done How Great Thou Art,
He still can wound you in the heart
To prove that heaven's master plan
Ignores the codes devised by man:
As God has shown from ancient days,
Omnipotence can cut both ways.
And if you think the dead can live,
Just know he'll take as well as give.
But if it's true that God is dead,
As *Time* and Nietzsche both have said,
No Lazarus will rise from death.
Those miracles? Don't hold your breath.

Church bells rang out at the news that 13 West Virginia miners, trapped for two days by an underground explosion in January 2006, had been rescued. The miracle story proved to be false.

Moving Pictures

The men who work the smoke machine
That gives the war its murky sheen
Call Michael Moore a demagogue
Because he blows away their fog.
"Moore twists the facts," the critics cry,
"He's unobjective, prone to lie,
Self-serving, rude and far too proud
To represent the unwashed crowd."

And yet at every multiplex,
It's not fake gunplay and tame sex,
Nor anesthetic Disney pap,
But this slob in his baseball cap
Who packs them in with *Fahrenheit*.
What chills the overheated right
Is not Moore's take on Nine One One —
It's that dissent's now date-night fun.

So all the neatly crafted schemes
To harness World Trade Center screams
And make the dead serve Bush's cause
Are torn to bits by this year's *Jaws*.
You say his aim is to deceive?
Look at the tangled webs you weave
Before you pick a film to pan —
And pray the kids choose *Spider-Man*.

Choice

The pro-life hit man's work is done:
At last he can put down his gun,
And use his faith for gentler ends
Than offing those whose work offends.
James Kopp will say his daily mass
And if he thinks the law's an ass,
He'll slowly let his feelings fade
And watch George Bush kill Roe v. Wade.

He hated blood, or so he said.
The man who shot a doctor dead
(Because he thought an unborn child
Was better served by men gone wild)
Feels bad that when his bullet tore
Through helpless flesh, the sight of gore
Corrupted his religious act,
And sanctified the doc he'd whacked.

America's a strange place, no?
A mass of cells *in utero*
Becomes the final battlefield
Where zealots hide behind God's shield.
It's life you love? Of course it's not.
What you love is the rifle shot
That silences those warring views,
And gives one man the right to choose.

James Kopp shot and killed Buffalo abortion provider Barnett Slepian in 1998. He was convicted of second-degree murder in 2003.

Deep in the Heart

If silly season seems more grave
Than usual, please blame the brave
And bold-as-brass dead soldier's mom
Who wouldn't let her grief stay mum.
Encamped outside the summer res
Of war's now largely absent Pres.,
Sad Cindy Sheehan mourns a son
Lost to a cause that can't be won
By leaders who ignore the dead
By clearing brush and going to bed.

To meet her in the Texas heat
Would be a statement of defeat
For George Bush and his coterie,
And clash with summer's reverie.
He drives by in his motorcade
To see folks who come ready-made
With thoughts identical to his,
And once again avoids her quiz:
"Just tell me, please, why did he die?"
The Texas tough guy turns his eye.

A Heapin' Spoonful

In Memoriam: Zal Yanovsky (1944–2002)
Rocker and Restaurateur

The songs don't age. On oldies shows,
The tunes that everybody knows
Still sound as perfect as they did
When you were just some crazy Yid
Who'd holed up in an East Side dive
And played guitar to stay alive.

Your stardom lasted, what, two years?
Instead of darting round in Lears,
And sipping chateau-bottled booze,
Or using proceeds from the blues,
To buy old castles in Provence,
And make those semi-yearly jaunts
To Madagascar or Mustique,
You quit when you were still a freak.

While Paul McCartney and The Stones
Kept sifting through rock's bleached-out bones,
You found a life beyond the charts
In berry crisps and Roquefort tartes,
And drew on Spoonful's sunny rays
To burn off Kingston's Waspy haze.

The life span of a rocker's brief,
But turning over each new leaf
Is not so simply done as said —
See Burton Cummings or the Dead.
You pulled it off: Your lemon buns
Match up with Billboard's Number Ones —
Who knew, back then, that *Daydream*'s boy
Would find new dreams to bring us joy?

The Pharaoh's Curse

Of all the wonders known to man,
There's nothing like the CT scan
To catch whatever's wrong with you,
If you've survived the nine-month queue.
And that's not all — your fatal pains,
Once diagnosed, give way to reigns
Of pharaohs who died long ago,
But died of what? We need to know,
And scanners in the mummy's tomb
Can tell us how he met his doom:
Just let the TV cameras roll,
And we'll sort body out from soul.

So much for King Tut's pyramid,
Which did no more than hide a kid,
While our advanced technology
Sheds light on Egyptology:
"Not murdered," our researchers say,
And Tut's remains are put away
To moulder for eternity.
Up next! Ramses' paternity
Determined by his DNA,
And proof that Cleopatra's gay,
From testing with an MRI
That shows how history's one big lie.

Scientists in a made-for-TV investigation used computerized tomography to explain the mystery of young King Tut's sudden death 3,300 years ago.

Citius, Altius, Fortius

How strange it is to be the jock
Who ends up as the one we mock
When papers print grand-jury leaks,
Or BALCO's Victor Conte speaks
To supplicants from ABC
Who want the lowdown on your pee.

One day your bulked-up bodies rule,
The next day it's "How dare you fool
The simple-minded populace?" —
Who never seemed to make a fuss
When our huge sluggers crushed the ball,
And our great runners thrashed the small.

Much like those lab-crowned queens and kings,
Capricious fortune has mood swings
That celebrate you till you're caught,
Then make you symbolize the rot
Of what's gone wrong with life today
When all you sought was bulked-up pay.

You're faster, higher, stronger now,
And when you win, we don't ask how,
Assuming that the right to know
Would compromise our inner glow.
So cheaters, just keep acting coy —
It's ignorance that brings us joy.

Whatever Sells

Just when you think things aren't so bad,
That now's the time to be a Dad
And put some meaning in your life
And, in a small way, soothe the strife
That makes us feel so all alone,
They have to go and make a clone.

Representatives of the
Raelians, a Montreal
religious cult, caused
a stir in 2002 by
announcing that they had
cloned the first human, a
baby girl named Eve.

Or so they say — We can't conceive
That scientists who all believe
Some aliens from outer space
Breathed life into the human race
From labs within their UFOs
Could go where no one boldly goes.

Is this the way new life begins?
Poor Baby Eve, conceived in sins
Too many to enumerate,
Will suffer just like Adam's mate
The stigma that's attached to those
Who undermine our godlike pose.

Much like her namesake, Eve makes clear
That virtue's just a sham veneer,
And lurking in the garden's weeds
Are demons that temptation feeds,
Emerging from the serpent's den
As breaking news on CNN.

Who needs a daughter, or a wife,
When you can buy eternal life?
So much for all the wise debate
Of stem-cell cures and beating fate.
Disease must wait when money talks:
Let's clone Ted Williams for the Sox!

Mission Accomplished

Who knows what, in the coming years,
The man who feeds his nation's fears
Will do to nourish hate abroad
And carry out the will of God?
Not George Bush, scary as he seems,
But Karl Rove, architect of dreams,
And warped boy genius of the right
Whose tricks secure election night.

Once, long ago, he babysat
The drunk, obnoxious frat-house brat
Who'd mastered all the deadly sins.
The rest is history: White House wins,
A leader who's so born-again
You'd think he hatched from God's own brain,
And eight long years to stretch the truth
Because Rove saved a misspent youth.

To members of the George Bush clan
Who like to talk straight, man to man,
Karl Rove's the "blossom in the turd,"
The wide-eyed, gung-ho backroom nerd
Who raked up muck and sifted crap
To make a rose-red victory map.
Why does he do it? Heaven knows,
But where shit happens, Karl Rove grows.

Blood Sport

How could you doubt that he's sincere?
When hockey stars squeeze out a tear
Across those massive bad-boy jaws
That dictate hockey's jungle laws,
Who thinks that they should do hard time?
Moist eyes can expiate a crime,
And prove that Todd Bertuzzi's nice,
Despite those moments on the ice
Denounced by interfering fools
Who don't get sport's unwritten rules —
In hockey, there's a higher truth,
Scarred eye for eye, false tooth for tooth.

All coaches know that it's no sin
To OD on adrenalin,
And though some no-names end up lame,
This killer urge defines our game,
And turns Vancouver's gentle Todd
Into the Bible's vengeful God.
One moment, ideal husband, dad,
The next, a well-meant punch turns bad.
"I didn't know I'd break his neck."
He didn't know? Well, what the heck —
Let justice turn a blinded eye,
And wait for someone else to die.

Him Again

Messiah-like unto the last,
Jacques Parizeau lives in the past
Where faith that's blind is worth much more
Than mundane ways of keeping score.
De temps en temps he reappears
To dig up all our buried fears,
And rouse the PQ's living dead
Who slumber in their quilted bed
With news Quebec could soon be free
If sovereigntists moved straight to *Oui* —
Why waste hopes on a plebiscite
When Jacques alone knows what is right?

Secession's now an old man's game,
A stick to prop the halt and lame
And batter anglos who'll vote No,
Or ethnics who aren't *comme il faut.*
Convinced this rainbow world's a mess?
Just pen an essay in *La Presse*
That says the system isn't fair
To those with *pure laine* underwear,
And though your views now seem deranged
We're glad, Jacques, that you never changed —
Lulled by that charmer Gilles Duceppe,
We missed your party's jackboot step.

Survivor: Iraq —
The Jessica Lynch Story

It's not war but its aftermath
That we must fear. Who knew the path
To terror's home, the oil-rich hell
They all said hid al-Qaeda's cell,
The endless search for poison gas
And bombs that made destruction mass,
Filmed battles that made strong men flinch,
Would lead at last to Private Lynch?

The face of war? It looks like this:
A wide-eyed, white-skinned heartland miss,
Blond hair topped with a chic beret —
An innocent in every way.
No wonder, then, that CBS
Would kill to sign up GI Jess,
And use the Humvee wounds she bore
To brighten up the fog of war.

A hero's welcome in the States
Means lawyers waiting at the gates
To ink you for that talk-show deal
Before your legs begin to heal —
"Who cares if she was really brave?
She'll look great sitting next to Dave."
And now we know what fighting's for:
So peace can be a bidding war.

John Kenneth Galbraith (1908–2006)

He knew the numbers always lied:
They left out money's moral side,
The greater good that wealth can bring
When goods are not the only thing.
For truth, look to his written word
Where economics turns absurd
When those who give their lives to stats
Ignore the public-housing rats,
The filthy air and dead-end schools,
To praise the fixed free-market rules.

The world is not a Harvard course:
He made light of the market's force,
For he well knew its "unseen hand"
Just means the bland will lead the bland.
But who still cares? All those tax cuts
That treat us as consumer sluts
Now mock his outsized farm-boy mind
With science of a dismal kind —
In place of Galbraith's bonhomie,
Quick cash and false economy.

The Class War

"We must uphold the rule of law,"
Says Gordon Campbell, he who saw
No harm in knocking back a few
And driving with his wits askew
While on vacation, far away
From any thoughts of teachers' pay.
Now this ex-drunk's our sober guide
To why some get an easy ride
On B.C.'s one-way gold-paved road,
While leaders simply shift the load
And make the teachers pay the price
Since public service is a vice.

Contracts imposed for years and years,
No wage increases — save the tears —
And here's a detail business likes:
You're too essential. No more strikes.
But it's not worth what Campbell saves
When public servants end up slaves,
Essential only in the court
That twists their rights into a tort.
Respect the law? Gord, what's at stake
Means more than some sweetheart tax break —
But if you like your tough-guy pose,
Try wage controls for CEOs.

Dear Leader

This evil axis — please explain
Why Baghdad's man is worse than Cain
And well deserves an awful fate
(Like death, or exile to a state
Where villas on the gin-soaked shores
Turn despots into harmless bores)
While North Korea gets away
With telling us we have to pay.

That Kim Jong-Il's one cagey guy.
No one will say that he should die
Or move to Paris, haunt the bars
And dictate only dull memoirs.
As George Bush says, "He starves his folks"
And, like all tyrants, shaves golf strokes,
Adjusting lies with fine aplomb.
There's just one thing: He has the Bomb.

Plutonium makes Kim seem nice —
Besides there's nothing there but ice,
And why shed blood on foreign soil
When there's no hope of finding oil?
And so, Dear Leader, we'll play dumb
And take our cue from David Frum
Who left you out of evil's gang.
Please rule in peace — we'll send you Tang.

You Don't Know Jack

Poor Jack Welch could do nothing wrong
When *Time* and *Fortune* sang his song:
The more jobs cut, the more plants razed,
The more his regal style was praised.
As long as GE's share price soared
It didn't matter who got gored,
And when time came to call it quits,
You think he had to use his wits
To get by on his pension plan?
You just don't know this clever man.

But someone did, and all too well.
Yes, much like Roman leaders fell,
Not fighting wars in far-off lands
But at their families' vengeful hands,
So Welch's plush retirement life
Was wrecked by his embittered wife,
Who, tired of his tomcatting ways,
Leaked details of his golden days:
On Wall Street, she made clear, success
Was just his ticket to excess.

By placing cronies on the board,
The savvy boss claimed his reward
And earned a life of constant treats:
A New York co-op, courtside seats,
Domingo singing at the Met,
Fresh flowers, servants, Boeing jet,
Full laundry service, HBO —
All paid for by the average Joe
Who watches GE's share price fall
While Neutron Jack is living tall.

It's tough to be a billionaire
With retribution in the air.
The lifestyle Jack Welch loved so well
Has been consigned to some new hell,
Where moneymakers hang their heads
And plutocrats are left for dead.
He's changed his tune: "I'll drop my perks —
Don't think I'm like those Enron jerks."
So is the bosses' boss contrite?
Jack Welch, the Teflon Man? Yeah, right.

On First Seeing Michelangelo's David, Newly Restored

An ageless beauty's lipo-ed hips,
Or old teeth bleached by Crest Whitestrips
To keep life's ravages at bay,
Would look less sleek, less present-day
Than David's heightened body parts,
Updated with the whitening arts.

The Renaissance now seems so old,
And ancient thinkers leave us cold,
But this is sculpture for our time:
Triumphant over dust and grime,
Young David fights off aging's lines
As easily as Philistines.

Five hundred years, and he's still buff.
Art's lesson? You can't cleanse enough,
So be like Michelangelo,
And worship beauty head to toe,
For who needs Art to give us Truth?
We'll settle for eternal youth.

America's God Blesses America

It's good to see you right on track.
You lost Me there a few years back
By seeking peace and shirking war —
Good God, man, what's the U.S. for?
Conceived in liberty and all,
You're quite the best thing since the Fall
Made mankind seem so second-rate.
But Eden now looks out-of-date,
A garden centre filled with weeds,
Compared to your brave words and deeds —
For in the years that Bush has reigned,
Your country's Paradise Regained.

America's now Number One:
Las Vegas can't be beat for fun,
Especially with the hookers gone,
Replaced by nice Céline Dion.
Deluxe health care and MRIs?
Your wealth's a sight for these sore eyes.
I always like a baseball game
But only when they sing My Name
Before the seventh-inning stretch.
Canadians? They make Me retch.
Those pinko, commie, peacenik dupes
Should bow and scrape before our troops.

Omnipotence, as you well know,
Is all one needs to fight a foe.
Forget about what others say —
You'll always have My A-OK,
And when you feel the urge to strike,
I've got to say: What's not to like?
You're up against the Heathen, right,
So bomb away all day and night
And when the smoke of battle clears,
You'll find that Allah's in arrears.
They roughed up pretty Private Lynch?
I'll make your victory a cinch.

And one last thing: Ignore the Pope —
The old guy doesn't have a hope.
He doesn't get you, never has,
He's plainsong to your free-form jazz.
Commandments are his daily bread,
But someone must avenge the dead.
As I told Moses way back when,
If there are lions in your den,
You can't sit back until they've won —
No, first we slay each first-born son
And only when we've killed the tots
Can we make time for thou-shalt-nots.

The Yellowed Jersey

To watch the great Lance Armstrong ride,
Must we ask what he's trying to hide,
And tell ourselves the human race
Can't keep up with his wicked pace?
To hear the boos and read the taunts
Inscribed along the Tour de France,
You'd think the man who outduels time
Had just pulled off the perfect crime,
As if a climb beyond compare
Were conjured from the Alps' thin air.
Each time he wins, the whispers start,
That Lance's cold and sullen art
Is crafted in a doctor's lab,
Which makes each race a snatch and grab,
A hero's triumph of the will,
With needles to subdue each hill.

It may be true. It may not be.
But fixed on that, we will not see
The tortured beauty of the Tour,
The moment when men know for sure
That choosing this inhuman ride
Means swearing off their human side,
And what the lifeless world calls sane
Will never match the joy of pain.
Sure, TV shows us Sheryl Crow
Attending to her Texas beau,
And for a moment we'll pretend
That Lance is everybody's friend.
Make no mistake: We're not alike
Once Armstrong climbs aboard his bike —
As mountains bend to each gear's shift,
So standards change and values drift.

Osama's Christmas Letter

The season's best to all of you
(Unless you're Christian, Kurd or Jew):
It's been a hectic time, I know,
For all who hate the foreign foe,
But here in hidden border caves
The past year's made us terror's slaves,
And while the mountain air's a perk,
Next year, for sure, I'm quitting work
To spend time with the wives and kids
And sell my memoirs — any bids?
Just kidding, folks. There's much to do
Before the killing season's through.
And what with all the bombs to buy,
And finding men who want to die
Because they heard the Prophet's call,
I doubt I'll make it to the mall
To get you each the perfect gift.
But just so no one feels too miffed,
Enclosed's my Christmas video:
Some say I could be Santa's bro'
But I'd prefer, this pagan feast,
To play the Wise Man from the East —
The beard and turban look just right
For holy war and Holy Night.
Instead of myrrh and precious gold,
My gifts will make the blood run cold,
With steel that severs guilty heads,
And lead that kills men in their beds,
And sends these sinners to the sky
To join their angels heard on high.
But those tales will be better told
When next year's corpse is growing cold.
So greetings, friends, and please take care,
From all of us in God-knows-where.

Chewing the Fat

"One Quarter-Pounder, minus bun."
It doesn't make lunch sound much fun,
Or do much for the hopes and schemes
Of Third World carbohydrate teams.
But, hey, the zeal to make carbs low
At least brought Atkins tons of dough,
And if his weight-loss scheme offends,
Who'll argue with the cast of *Friends*?

So what if Atkins was obese?
We live life on a short-term lease
Where every day might be the last,
And there's no time to stop and fast.
You want your doc to look the part?
Might just as well insist that art
Be made by those who live their themes
And don't have secret get-rich dreams.

Who needs to lose weight? Once you're dead,
Eternity leaves you unfed,
And when you're buried in the ground
It won't be hard to shed a pound.
Until then all that low-carb beer
Can only feed a life of fear,
So pass the pot of Special Sauce,
And let's toast make-believe weight loss.

New Brooms
or The Dust Heap of History

Why can't it all be cut and dried?
We'd like to say Jean Chrétien lied,
And that the mess of sponsorship
Was firmly held within his grip —
That he was just some small-town thug
Who flew too high on power's drug,
And stole our virtue while we snoozed,
But still won't act like the accused.

We'd like the past to go away,
And with no dragons left to slay,
We'd start anew, carte blanche, clean slate,
To cure our misbegotten state.
But then we see Paul Martin's face,
And doubts return: You can't erase
What went before, or style the past
To suit the new flag on your mast.

They didn't know. Unless they did.
And who'd they ever hope to kid
By telling us that moral strength
Is shown when sleaze stays at arm's length?
Paul's arms were longer, Jean's more short,
But don't search Gomery's report
To find who was the better man,
Or who'll end up the also-ran.

William Westmoreland (1914–2005)

Old soldiers never die, they say,
But as Westmoreland fades away
And joins in heaven's body counts,
The death toll of young soldiers mounts,
Which shows those lines on growing old
Mean nothing when fresh limbs go cold.

Old generals get to slip away,
Despite the blood they shed at Hue,
But their ideas, alas, don't die.
They soldier on, to fill the sky
Above Baghdad with "shock and awe"
As awful as what Vietnam saw.

"Let no one doubt: We've got it made."
With every payload, each air raid,
You prove to them that might means right,
And soon they must give up the fight —
For who'll defeat technology
Armed just with ideology?

When optimism goes to war,
All gung-ho spirit to the core,
True patriots claim victory
Before they read their history.
Westmoreland's lesson? Still not learned,
And once again the tide has turned.

Putin's Progress

Well, yes, he is ex-KGB,
And if he lets a wedge of Brie
Submit before his sharpened knife,
Or downs some pinot with his wife
In crystal hand-blown for the czar,
Make no mistake: This spook's come far.
But deep inside, or not so deep,
He's still that cold, police-state creep.

In Putin's modicum of charm
Presides the happy face of harm,
And even though he'll never match
Joe Stalin's longing to dispatch
A million here, a million there,
Vlad still intends to do his share:
To prove a leader must be cruel,
He'll sacrifice a far-off school.

For those who think that Russia's seed
Must kill off every foreign weed,
The holy truth does not come cheap:
As you have sown, so shall you reap.
Go finger terror's bogeyman,
Deflect the blame, because you can,
And show yourself a man of taste,
While children pay for Grozny's waste.

The Same Old Song: 2005

Our guiding light's George W.
Who lends a touch of déjà vu,
A been-there, done-that sense of fate,
To those of us who contemplate
The residue of hope and fear
That adds up to another year.
This President in cruise control,
Who drives the straight line to his goal
And only likes to see what's best,
Wants each year to be like the rest —
Predictable, immune from change,
It's life lived in a narrow range
Where nothing's going to cause surprise,
And bad news can't offend the eyes.
Katrina, as you may recall,
With all its power to appall
Could not begin to penetrate
The levees of his mental state,
And when he had to pick a judge,
How hard it was to make him budge
From looking at the chosen few
Who'd never make a year seem new.
But if George Bush has set the tone,
It's not like it's just him alone
Who makes us want to count the days
Until the world can mend its ways.
Please ponder how the Papal See,
Whose timeline is eternity,
When asked to find another pope,
Considered change and then said, "Nope,"
Or how Tom Cruise, the ageless hunk,
Stayed true to L. Ron Hubbard's bunk
And found himself that *Dawson's* wraith
To share his baby and his faith
(And put to rest, we hope, the thought
That Tom is something that he's not).

But speaking of recycled trash
That tabloids use to make their cash,
This year could never be complete
Till we've brought up Brad's itchy feet,
Which fled Jen's domesticity
For Angelina, *plus jolie*,
And proved, when you've got looks and fame,
That nothing has to stay the same.
The rest of us, alas, are stuck
With lifelines fenced by fate and luck —
By which I mean, dear kids and wife,
I couldn't have a better life,
And only now and then aspire
To fuel Belinda Stronach's fire
Or wish, if fortune played more fair,
That I had Stephen Harper's hair
(Which much like him, shows no effect
When winds of change try to deflect
The hair-sprayed order of our lives
To make the mess where freedom thrives).
But since the truth's both plain and bald,
Just let me say I'm quite appalled
That his dark forces of the right
Could steal the next election night —
But something also makes me guess,
For all his talk, that he'll be less
Inclined to push for real change,
Once he's pushed news crews out of range.
(I must confess I made this fix
Four months into Two Thousand Six
In hopes that when one leader's gone,
The new one prompts the same old yawn.)
So *plus ça change*, yet who's to blame
When mortals flit back to the flame?

"Charles Weds Camilla" — call that news?
Iran's new leader can't stand Jews,
The CIA has bent the rules,
The U.S. envoy says we're fools
To challenge their God-given right
To win an age-old lumber fight,
Some teenage hockey star is god,
A thug makes our Olympic squad,
Top CEOs end up as crooks,
And Peter Newman still sells books
By nodding at Mulroney's guff —
It sure sounds like the same old stuff.
Dull minds that don't learn from the past
Repeat it to the very last,
But don't despair in these dark days,
For things at least have changed for gays
Who couldn't stand the status quo
Where weddings must be hetero:
In one year, look how far they came,
Through marriage where the sex is same.

The Eternal Lament

For Leaf fans, hockey's pains don't stop —
While waiting for the puck to drop
To start another hopeful year,
We pack away our playoff gear
(The flags that flew from each car door,
The face paint of the true hard-core,
Tie Domi's sweater — note the blood —
Those crates of beer named Blue or Bud),
And try to figure why this team,
As always, "just ran out of steam,"
To use the well-worn sports cliché
That comes in handy every May.

So question Sundin's inner fire
And join the "sack-the-GM" choir —
It's true the Stanley Cup goes on,
But who can watch a game till dawn,
Or search the screens in die-hard bars
For overtime's unlikely stars,
When teams named after sharks and ducks
Find favour with the god of pucks.
We'd rather do our taxes, thanks,
Or watch Meg Ryan and Tom Hanks,
Than spend our sleepless hockey time
On *Hockey Night* in Anaheim.

Olive Branch

The key for tyrants — Simply last,
And everyone forgets your past,
Or at the very least forgives.
So millions died? Gadhafi lives,
And though he's absolutely mad,
These days he doesn't look half-bad
(Once you get past that coal-black hair)
Beside the rest from evil's lair:
Weird Kim Jong-Il, the Taliban,
Those backward mullahs in Iran,
Al-Qaeda's push, Hamas's shove,
And let's not mention Courtney Love.
Like bad-boy rappers as they age,
He's gone from gangsta thug to sage,
And what once filled his White House file
Now seems the very height of style:
Girl bodyguards arrayed in pearls,
A fez perched on his flowing curls,
The desert tent pitched on the lawn
Where EU ministers can fawn,
And tell him that their lust for oil
Has taken vengeance off the boil.
Compared, let's say, to Tony Blair,
He brings a welcome dash of flair,
And who can keep up hate for long,
When Libya hints it acted wrong.
He may have tripped the West's alarms
But now he wants to buy our arms,
So let's ignore all those he killed,
Provided that he pays when billed.

Perdita in Perdition

In sport, unlike the finer arts,
You can't revise your stumbling starts
And wait until your form's just right
Before you brave the world's cruel sight.
It's all up front — the highs, the lows,
The did-my-bests and I-don't-knows
When some guy from the CBC
Seeks words to match your misery.

You let us down? No, not at all.
The hurt we feel when athletes fall,
The shame done to the maple leaf,
Depends much more on hype than grief;
If you've destroyed a nation's hope,
Have Dick Pound test *our* pee for dope,
Or check what other altered state
Makes couch hogs call you second-rate.

"Perdita (fem.): a loss or waste."
No, not at all. This test you faced
Will be the hurt that makes you strong,
And just as surely prove us wrong
For thinking it's a tragic sin
When those we worshipped didn't win.
A wise Greek wrote: In drama's art,
The beauty's in the painful part.

Whale Song

They buried Willy — not at sea,
Where death at last lets whales float free,
But in a grave on driest land,
Still answering the crowd's command
To prove an orca has a soul
Immured in his eternal hole.

They called you Keiko ("Lucky One"),
A name that dignified your fun
And made a theme park's killer toy,
The nature lovers' pinup boy —
Where Moby-Dick once dodged harpoons,
You prompted Michael Jackson tunes.

Enslaved, you played the role of God;
But men knew better: Find your pod,
And you could start a new career
Where certainty gave way to fear,
And dull routine made room for doubt.
They set you free — your luck ran out.

Good Will Toward Men

For God so loved the world, he sent
His one and only Son, who spent
The Christmas season at the mall
Before he died to save us all.
That shopping's blessed by God's own word
Is in the Bible, so I've heard,
And this is why, each holiday
We must do things the Christian way:
Be rude to those who send a card
From which the name of Christ's been barred,
And tell the President that he
Betrayed true Christianity
By purging Jesus from the notes
He sends to those who gave him votes.

If someone puts a pine or fir
On public land, we won't defer
And let them make our sacred tree
A symbol of diversity,
But fight the good fight till it's done,
And our God's forced on everyone.
This "Season's Greetings" stuff must stop
For Jesus to come out on top,
And when we've made clerks at the store
Say "Merry Christmas," there's still more:
Max out your Visa, praise the Lord,
But don't forget the angel's sword
That leaves the infidels afraid —
Let's make Iraq our new Crusade.

In the holiday season of 2005, conservative Christian groups attacked the White House for sending out greeting cards that omitted the word Christmas.

The Body Politic
Leni Riefenstahl (1902–2003)

We now see evil as banal,
No thanks to Leni Riefenstahl.
Her lens turned misfits into gods,
And Calvin Kleined those Aryan bods
To make the heroes Germans craved —
For how could beauty be depraved?
By bringing style to war's debris,
She found art's fearful symmetry.

No need to ask just what she knew
About the fate of any Jew —
In loving shots of Nazi abs,
She blessed all fascist power grabs.
To pretty up the master race
Should be a sure route to disgrace,
And yet her legacy lives on
Wherever beauty plays its con —
All those sucked in by looks that kill
Are cheering *Triumph of the Will.*

Last Judgments

The lives described in death's small ads
Show loving wives and doting dads
Who wouldn't dream of doing wrong,
Who never cursed the Falun Gong
For blocking sidewalks when they jogged,
And didn't drive with windshields fogged
Or watch the porn on pay-TV
If it meant others then could see
Their lives weren't orderly and dull —
Safe Ottawa, not risky Hull.

There's comfort in an ordered end:
It means we all have time to mend
The ragged quilt we call our ways.
Soon death will bring us better days,
Where illnesses are bravely borne
And no one earns the boss's scorn,
Where every war's a hero's chance
To triumph at life's victory dance,
And there is nothing left to do
But give thanks to the ICU.

Religions say the afterlife
Is where we go to end this strife.
Excuse me, but eternal rest
Would seem to lack a certain zest,
And if it's paradise you seek
Look here, right now, today, this week.
Death's not the thing that we should fear —
It's living life in second gear.
So go ahead, start acting bad.
We'll fix it in the final ad.

Prisoner X's Postcard Home

Guantanamo's a pleasant spot
To while your teenage years away.
The breezes blow, the weather's hot
The sky is blue, or so they say.

The guards insist I've gained some weight
And look more like a Yankee now.
There's more good news: My mental state
Is much improved with better chow.

Before, unfed, in desert rags,
I really wasn't very nice.
But here, far from al-Qaeda nags,
I'm finding peace in lamb and rice.

Please, don't believe the rumour mill
That says we all crave suicide.
Our love of life is hard to kill,
And only three of us have died.

Instead of pain, they use rewards
To get us all to spill the beans,
Much better than shock-treatment wards
In Egypt or the Philippines.

Interrogation's not so bad.
'Round here, we call it "torture lite."
Just give them tips about your Dad,
And then they'll let you sleep at night.

A year in jail feels like a day —
It's heaven after Kabul's hell.
Back there I dozed on dirty hay,
But here I've got my own mesh cell.

So who needs lawyers or a court?
My fate can wait another year.
Who knows? By then, this Navy fort
Might serve us chicken wings and beer.

P.S. Don't fret about my rights.
I'm sure that you've done all you could.
I miss you in the long, dark nights —
[This line's blacked out for prisoner's good].

To a Poet Laureate

Your head feels heavy with that crown?
Don't let those laurels weigh you down,
Or pull you into Rideau's weeds
Where those who write of human needs
Become the bogged-down slaves of pomp.
To beautify that Bytown swamp
Takes more than poets have to give.
Who needs their offer? Why not live
A life that's free from compromise,
A laureate of truth, not lies.

As if you would accept advice
From hacks like me — You rolled the dice
And said on balance you could do
More good than harm, remaining true
To principles of poetry
While sampling Sussex Drive's fine Brie,
And bring the wit of Donne or Pope
To odes that hymn the war on dope.
Just kidding — given what they pay,
I bet they'll let you have your way.

But which way do your verses tend?
Are you that willing to offend
The people that you're hired to serve
By crowding them with your best curve?
Or do you think the poet's job
Is just to toss an easy lob,
And turn the country's cries and screams
Into a feel-good *Field of Dreams*?
Depends on where you want renown —
In Rideau Hall or Cooperstown.

It's hard to say. I've read your stuff,
And while I'd never call it fluff
(Your writing's agile and alert)
There's little that could ever hurt
The listless masters of our fate
Who pay the poet's going rate.
You'll craft fine anthems on the dole,
And doubtless plumb the nation's soul,
But don't forget, while we're beguiled —
Penned salmon can't compare with wild.

Acknowledgements

Poetry can be a solitary activity, which is why I'm more than usually grateful to my wonderful colleagues at *The Globe and Mail* for their companionship, curiosity and all-round ability to stand there while I babble on—Liam Lacey and Rick Groen have proved particularly willing to take as well as give over the years. Poetic Justice appears in the paper's Focus section, where both Jerry Kinoshita and Alison Gzowski have helped sharpen my sometimes hazy visions. Focus editor Jerry Johnson, an optimist against all the odds, has the gift for making impossible things seem possible and even strangely enjoyable. Cathrin Bradbury, who first encouraged me to write these poems, has always been a force for risk-taking and an enthusiast in the face of doubts, not all of them mine. Carl Wilson has been the perfect editor for a deadline poet—quick, funny, to the point and wise. In the wider *Globe*, Sylvia Stead has helped ease the transition from printed page and database to book form, and Patrick Martin came to the rescue at a low point with his usual eloquence and calm.

This book came into being because of Lionel Koffler, and his unstoppable belief that these poems were made to last. He and his team at Firefly Books, including Michael Worek, Ian Murray and Barbara Campbell, have managed to be both fast at putting together this late-breaking volume and patient when my speed couldn't keep up with theirs. I'm especially glad they could persuade Brian Gable to contribute the illustrations.

At Westwood Creative Artists, I must salute Bruce Westwood for his once and future labours, and John Pearce, who heads up the diminishing-returns division of Allemang Inc.

My friend Ken Roberts once described me as a "renegade jock." I'd like to thank him for steering me from concussive bodychecks toward the verbal arts, and acknowledge other friends and teachers who've put poetic ideas in my head: Donald Gutteridge, Stephen Perry, Don Schmitt, Peter Bell, Elaine Fantham, David Wistow, Kerry Skinner, Alan Toff and Michael Lloyd. And not to forget Clive James, who first made me think about writing rhymes.

Closer to home, poetry means late dinners above all. My gratitude to my wife, Patricia Holtz, extends infinitely beyond her willingness to wait while the words fall into place, but at the time this always seems like one of her greatest attractions. Her love of Auden and Donne as well as baseball and banter makes our own rhyming couplet even stronger.

And to my clever children, Sam and Liz: Who could have guessed that our Easter-egg hunts would turn into this?

Index of Poems

Date in brackets following title indicates when poem appeared in *The Globe and Mail*.